GALE
CENGAGE Learning

Novels for Students, Volume 3

Copyright © 1998
Gale Research
835 Penobscot Building
645 Griswold St.
Detroit, MI 48226-4094

This book is printed on acid-free paper that meets the minimum requirements of American National Standard for Information Sciences—Permanence Paper for Printed Library Materials, ANSI Z39.48-1984.

ISBN 0-7876-2113-7
ISSN 1094-3552

Printed in the United States of America.
10 9 8 7 6 5 4

Grendel

John Gardner 1971

Introduction

Completed in 1970 and published the following year, *Grendel* was the first of John Gardner's novels to bring him not just critical but popular success. The novel was praised as a literary *tour de force* and named a book of the year by *Time Newsweek* magazines. As a professor of English specializing in medieval literature, Gardner had been teaching *Beowulf,* the source of inspiration for *Grendel,* for many years at various colleges. A relatively minor character in *Beowulf,* Grendel is a symbol for "darkness, chaos, and death," according to critic John M. Howell in *Understanding John Gardner.* In

Gardner's version, however, Grendel becomes a three-dimensional character with, in Howell's words, "a sense of humor and a gift for language." Grendel even has a weakness for poetry. As a would-be artist, Grendel strives, however comically, to escape from his baseness. Such is the power of art, Gardner seems to be saying, that even a monster can be affected by it. Gardner also develops the theme of heroism as another moral force that enables society to advance by elevating Unferth, a minor character in the original poem, to a major character and foil for Grendel. Similarly, Gardner builds up the role of Grendel's mother to emphasize, through her inarticulateness, the importance of language in the development of civilization. Gardner also creates a relationship between Grendel and the dragon (another minor character in the original epic) in order to expand the concept of nihilism—the belief that there is no purpose to existence. Through these changes, Gardner is able to develop themes that recur not only in *Grendel* but throughout his other works: the struggle between good and evil, the clash between order and disorder, the hero's sacrifice and achievement of immortality, and the importance of art and the artist as a means of affirming the moral meaning of life.

Author Biography

Grendel reflects two of Gardner's major interests: his belief in fiction as a moral force for good, and his passion for the medieval period in history. Gardner was born in 1933 and grew up in Batavia, New York. His mother was an English teacher and his father a farmer and lay preacher, so it is perhaps not surprising that Gardner was eventually drawn to the medieval period, when society was largely agricultural and the Church played a central role in life. As a boy he was attracted not only to language but also to music and chemistry. His father's passion for opera rubbed off on young John, who sang in various choirs as a boy and later wrote several opera libretti on medieval subjects. Having decided that English was his field because he did well at it, Gardner attended DePauw University from 1951 to 1953. The latter year he also married Joan Louise Patterson, with whom he had two children. Transferring to Washington University in St. Louis, Gardner received his A.B. in 1955. He also took an M.A. at the State University of Iowa in 1956 and a Ph.D. in 1958. As his doctoral dissertation, Gardner wrote an unpublished novel, *The Old Men.*

After receiving his Ph.D., Gardner pursued a teaching career while continuing his writing. He held positions at a number of colleges and universities before settling at Southern Illinois University from 1965 to 1974. His first published novel, *The Resurrection*, was published in 1966, though it attracted little notice, and his second, *The Wreckage of Agathon*, appeared in 1970. Gardner had been writing fiction fairly steadily from an early age, and he described *Grendel* (1971) as a "late work" in an interview in 1974. Though *The Sunlight Dialogues* (1972) and *October Light* (1976) were published after *Grendel*, both were actually written prior to it. *Grendel* was the first book to bring Gardner widespread recognition. The novel was named one of the ten best books of 1971 by *Time* and *Newsweek*.

During this period the author also published (with Lennis Dunlap) a textbook, *The Forms of Fiction* (1961); a translation, *The Complete Works of the Gawain-Poet* (1965); *Jason and Medeia* (1972), a novel in verse; the collection *The King's Indian: Stories and Tales* (1974); and other scholarly works on medieval literary subjects.

Both *The Sunlight Dialogues* and *Nickel Mountain* (1973) were well received by the popular press. *October Light* won the National Book Critics Circle Award for fiction and was named one of the best books of 1976 by both *Time* and the *New York Times*. Gardner's reputation went down, however, after the publication of *On Moral Fiction* in 1978. While stating his own philosophy of moral affirmation eloquently, to many critics the book seemed arrogant and dismissive of many of Gardner's contemporaries.

From 1974 to 1978, Gardner held several short-term appointments in New York and New

England colleges. During this period and the following four years, Gardner also published poetry, scholarly and children's books, a novel titled *Mickelsson's Ghosts* (1982), and a collection of stories. In 1978, he founded the writing program at the State University of New York at Binghamton. He served as its director until the time of his death, in a motorcycle accident, in 1982.

Background: The Epic Beowulf

John Gardner's *Grendel* is a retelling of the first part of the Anglo-Saxon epic, *Beowulf,* with an important difference. In *Grendel,* the monster gets to tell the story. Because this is a retelling, however, Gardner assumes that his reader is familiar with the story of *Beowulf.* Indeed, without such familiarity the reader would be lost. Accordingly, the following is a very brief summary of the Anglo-Saxon story.

Beowulf is the oldest long poem in English, written as early as perhaps the seventh century A.D., with the only manuscript version dating to around 1000 A.D. The Danish King, Hrothgar, has built a fabulous meadhall, Heorot, for himself and his retainers. However, Heorot is not safe: each night the monster Grendel attacks the hall and kills Hrothgar's men. Beowulf, a Geat, hears of Hrothgar's distress and travels the land of the Danes to help rid Heorot of the monster and to garner fame for himself.

Beowulf fights with Grendel when the monster attacks the hall. He rips off Grendel's arm, and the monster flees, dying. Grendel's mother later attacks Hrothgar's men in retaliation for her son's death. Beowulf also fights Grendel's mother and kills her.

In the last section of *Beowulf,* set some fifty

years later, old Beowulf, now king of the Geats, does battle with a gold-hoarding dragon who has been savaging the Geats. In this final battle, Beowulf and the dragon kill each other.

Chapters 1-4: Grendel and the World

Gardner's *Grendel* is a book of twelve chapters, the number recalling Grendel's twelve-year battle with Hrothgar, the months of the year, and the signs of the zodiac. The book, however, is not in straight chronological order. Rather, Gardner uses devices such as flashbacks, allusions, and foreshadowing to help relate the story. The present tense passages of the book move the reader chronologically through the twelve months of the twelfth year of Grendel's war with Hrothgar. Interspersed among the present tense passages are past tense passages telling of the years leading up to the present. Throughout, as the first person narrator of his own story, Grendel grows in his understanding of the nature of language and its power to create and destroy worlds.

The book opens in April, the month of the ram. It is in the present tense with Grendel observing the world around him, watching a ram on a mountain. Immediately his concern with language becomes evident: "Talking, talking. Spinning a web of words, pale walls of dreams, between myself and all I see."

Grendel lives in a cave under a burning lake with his mother, a mute, beast-like creature who cares for and protects him. There are other "shadowy shapes" in the cave, but Grendel alone can speak. In Chapter 2, Grendel recalls an important moment: trapped in a tree, crying for his mother, Grendel encounters men for the first time. The most important thing about the encounter is that the men speak words that Grendel understands, although the men do not understand Grendel's words.

After his rescue from the tree by his mother, Grendel begins watching the men and their actions. The third chapter is a summary of what he sees throughout the years as the Danes slowly develop human civilization. Hrothgar becomes the most powerful of the kings, because, Grendel tells the reader, he has a theory about the purpose of war that makes his battles effective.

About this time a blind poet arrives at Hrothgar's hall. The poet is called the Shaper. The Shaper does more than make poetry, according to Grendel. Through his retelling of Hrothgar's history, "The man had changed the world, had torn up the past by its thick, gnarled roots and had transmuted it, and they who knew the truth remembered it his way—and so did I." The Shaper's arrival is particularly significant for Grendel. In his songs, he names Grendel as one of the race of Cain, a representative of all that is dark and evil. For Hrothgar's men and for Grendel himself, this is what he becomes.

Chapters 5-7: The Dragon, Unferth, and Wealtheow

Grendel, unhinged by the Shaper's words, visits the dragon to find answers to his questions about order, language, and truth. (This is the same dragon who will kill and be killed by Beowulf in the Anglo-Saxon epic.) The dragon tells him that the Shaper's words are an "illusion of reality," and that they only serve to make the men think that there is meaning in the universe. According to the dragon, the men's religion, ritual, and songs are nothing more than nonsense whose only purpose it to make them believe that life is not random accident. The dragon denies the existence of God and meaning, advising Grendel to "seek out gold and sit on it."

Grendel discovers after leaving the dragon that the dragon has put a curse on him: he cannot be injured by the men's weapons. He begins raiding Hrothgar's meadhall, killing and eating men. On one occasion, he encounters Unferth, who stands up to him with bold words of heroism. Unferth's goal is to make his reputation by either killing or being killed by the monster. Grendel, instead of fighting, answers in words, and Unferth is shaken to realize that Grendel has language. Grendel engages in banter until Unferth, in frustration, says, "No more talk!" and rushes him with his sword. Uninjured, Grendel responds by throwing apples at him. By behaving in this unexpected way, Grendel completely humiliates Unferth. As a further insult, Grendel does not kill Unferth, but leaves him to his shame. Later, Unferth tracks Grendel to his lair and there confronts him on the meaning of heroism. Grendel demonstrates to Unferth that life is indeed meaningless by refusing to engage him in combat. Instead, he returns Unferth to the hall, kills two guards, and in future raids, spares Unferth's life. As Grendel reports, "So much for heroism."

In the next chapter, Grendel reveals in flashback the circumstances of the arrival of Wealtheow, the Queen at Hrothgar's court, during the second year of his raiding. At that time, Hrothgar was at war with the Helmings, Wealtheow's people. Her brother offered her to Hrothgar as a means of weaving a peace. Wealtheow's name means "holy servant of common good," and her role in *Beowulf as* well as *Grendel* is clearly that. Grendel attacks the hall and the Queen, but decides not to kill her.

Chapters 8-12: Grendel's End

In the eighth chapter, Grendel relates how Hrothgar's nephew, Hrothulf, arrived at the meadhall after the murder of his father. His resentful attitude and desire for power gives Grendel the opportunity to consider "the idea of violence" which grows in the young man. The following chapter features Grendel's encounter with a priest, which leads to several observations on the nature of religion. In the tenth chapter, Grendel feels tormented by boredom, and observes the death of the old poet Shaper. Meanwhile, his mother has become strangely protective of him and tries to prevent Grendel from leaving the lair.

In the next-to-last chapter, strangers arrive by sea. This is the unnamed hero that the reader knows to be Beowulf. Grendel is strangely excited by the presence of the strangers. He attacks the hall late at night and makes a fatal error: he allows Beowulf to grab him by the wrist. Beowulf tells him about the cycles of existence. Although everything in this world will be destroyed, something will remain and will grow again. Although Grendel cannot be harmed by steel weapons, he is killed by the strength of Beowulf's grip. Beowulf rips off Grendel's arm at the shoulder socket. Grendel screams again for his mother, then staggers to edge of his cliff. To the end, he attributes his death to random accident. As he falls into death and over the cliff, he says to the animals watching him, "Poor Grendel's had an accident." The last words of the novel are enigmatic: *"So may you all."* Whether this is curse or a prediction is unclear. Grendel, however, dies.

Characters

Beowulf

Beowulf is the hero with the "strength of thirty thanes" (Chapter 10) who finally slays Grendel and brings peace to the land of the Scyldings. Significantly, Beowulf's coming is not only prophesied by the old woman who speaks of a "giant across the sea" but is also alluded to in the dying words of the Shaper: "I see a time when the Danes once again——." Beowulf's arrival is also foretold by the lengthening of the days, which is a traditional sign of hope and new life. When Beowulf, the son of Ecgtheow, lands among the Danes, he introduces himself and his party as Geats who are "hearthcompanions of King Hygilac" (Chapter 11). Beowulf has come specifically to kill Grendel, but Hrothgar's court realizes, of course, that whoever slays the monster will no doubt soon have a fair claim to the land of the Scyldings and Helmings as well. When Beowulf finally confronts Grendel, he tricks the monster into thinking he is asleep with the other thanes (warriors) in the mead hall. Beowulf then grabs Grendel's arm and twists it behind the monster, which slips in a pool of blood he himself has created in slaughtering weaker thanes. After forcing Grendel to acknowledge his own mortality by commanding him to "sing of walls" (Chapter 12), Beowulf rips off Grendel's arm, and the monster dies from loss of blood. While carrying out this deed, Beowulf intones these lines: *"Though you murder the world ... strong searching roots will crack your cave and rain will cleanse it: The world will burn green, sperm build again. My promise. Time is the mind, the hand that makes (fingers on harpstrings, hero-swords, the acts, the eyes of queens). By that I kill you. "* Thus does Beowulf catalogue all the acts that he believes are stronger than the forces of evil, alluding to all the characters in the story who have acted in the common good—including the Shaper, Unferth, and Wealtheow.

Dragon

The Dragon, who first appears in Chapter 5, may be real or just another figment of Grendel's imagination. Nevertheless, it plays an important role in the story as an exemplar of a philosophy of nihilism (the idea that existence is meaningless), solipsism (the idea that only the self exists), and chaos. The dragon's advice to Grendel—"Seek out gold—but not my gold—and guard it!" (stated twice in the chapter)—only begins to suggest his cynical view of the world. For the dragon, there is no real meaning in life, only accidental incidents, each one a "foolish flicker-flash in the long dull fall of eternity." While the Dragon himself claims to be able to see all space and time (however weary he is of the sight), ordinary mortals must struggle along with their illusions of connection, meaning, and reality. Nevertheless, the Dragon's power is such that after meeting him, Grendel is impervious to the weapons of men (Chapter 6).

First priest

The high priest Ork's company includes four other priests who serve under him. The first priest focuses on the words of the gospel, not the philosophy behind them. He is especially fond of quoting scripture to support every thought and action. Thus, when Ork says that he has seen Grendel—"The Great Destroyer"—the first priest replies: "Blasphemy! It is written, 'Ye shall not see my face'" (Chapter 9).

Fourth priest

Only the fourth priest, who is younger than the others, seems genuinely moved by Ork's responses to Grendel's questions about the nature of the "king of the Gods" and the meaning of life. Somewhat comically, the younger man exclaims, "The rhythm is re-established! Merely rational thought... leaves the mind incurably crippled.... But now at last, sweet fantasy has found root in your blessed soul!" (Chapter 9) and *"The gods made this world for our joy!"* (Chapter 10).

Freawaru

She is Hrothgar's daughter by "a woman who'd died" (Chapter 8). Hrothulf blushes whenever she speaks to him, indicating a fondness for her. Hrothgar, however, plans to marry her off to the ruler of another rival fiefdom.

Grendel

While the monster Grendel was a less important character than Beowulf in the Old English epic on which Gardner's novel is based, as the title character here he has become the star attraction. Grendel is violent, cruel, cynical, and degenerate—in short, monstrous. Yet, like the humans who speak a similar language to his, Grendel has feelings, too. Like any mother's child, he cries when he is caught in the tree trunk (Chapter 2). Most important, he is moved by the words of the Shaper—the human poet whose words, though they no doubt embellish the truth, yet live through time to change the world and inspire the Scyldings to do great deeds (Chapter 3). Grendel is a monster, yet uses language as humans do, to try to define and explore his world.

As narrator, Grendel recounts the story of his life from birth to death. His search for meaning in his existence takes him to the home of the dragon and drives him to spy on the meadhall of Hrothgar. But when Grendel, inspired by the Shaper, tries to join the human race by leaving the "dark side" to which he believes he has been banished, he is misunderstood and turned on by fearful men. As a result, Grendel reverts to his former nihilism—believing there is no purpose to existence. He becomes vengeful, though remaining haunted by the Shaper's words.

Media Adaptations

- *Grendel* was adapted as an animated cartoon titled *Grendel, Grendel, Grendel* by Alexander Stitt in 1981. Sir Peter Ustinov was featured as the voice of Grendel.

Grendel is the author of numerous acts of violence and cruelty. By telling events from his point of view, however, the monster is still able to elicit sympathy from the reader. This sympathy has led some critics and readers to consider Grendel as the "hero" of the novel. Careful consideration of the entire text, however, allows for a different interpretation.

Grendel's mother

She has no name, and may be only a dim

memory in Grendel's mind rather than an actual living character in the story. Yet Grendel's mother plays an important role as the monster's comforter and savior. She also serves to highlight the importance of language in the novel. Grendel's mother communicates only in inarticulate sounds that even Grendel cannot understand—although he often says, and then denies, that her sounds might mean something. The shadowy cave where Grendel's mother dwells represents her ignorance. Similarly, the bone pile she is constantly picking through suggests that those without the ability to communicate are left to scraps of others. Although Grendel's mother does not possess language, unlike her son she seems to have found some purpose in life: as Grendel says, "I was, in her eyes, some meaning I could never know and might not care to know" (Chapter 2).

Halga the Good

The younger brother of Hrothgar, Halga the Good is murdered, leaving his son Hrothulf to reside as an orphan in Hrothgar's court.

Herogar

The king of a neighboring fiefdom to that of Hrothgar (Chapter 1).

Holy servant of common good

See Wealtheow

Hrothgar

King of the Scyldings, he first appears in the story as a tall man in a long black beard who inspects the tree in which Grendel is trapped (Chapter 2). When Grendel shouts at Hrothgar and his men, Hrothgar throws an ax at the monster, who is finally saved by his mother. Hrothgar gradually learns that the secret to power is not killing your neighbors but collecting tribute from them and making them your allies. He also is smart enough to build roads to connect his fiefdoms and bring peace and order to formerly warring bands. Finally, when threatened by Hymgod of the Helmings, neighbors who are potentially more powerful than he, Hrothgar realizes that the solution to his problem is to accept Hymgod's offer of his sister, Wealtheow, as his bride. In the twilight of his rule, Hrothgar is subjected to the trials of various forms of political philosophy—from the traditional heroism of the feudalistic age, seen in his Hrothgar's subject Unferth, to the Machiavellian beliefs and anarchism of his young nephew Hrothulf and his mentor Red Horse (a pun on the name of the radical French philosopher Georges Sorel).

Hrothulf

One of Halga the Good's two sons, Hrothulf comes at the age of fourteen to live at Hrothgar's mead hall after the death of his father. He is sullen and brooding: "already a God-damned pretender," Grendel observes (Chapter 8). Though exposed to the philosophy of anarchism by his mentor, Red Horse, Hrothulf is not totally taken in by the old man's violent beliefs. "Nobody in his right mind would praise violence for its own sake, regardless of its ends," says Hrothulf (Chapter 8). Perhaps more telling, Hrothulf remains kind to his young cousins, the children of Hrothgar and Wealtheow, though they stand ahead of him in line to the kingship.

Hygmod

Hrothgar's challenger from a neighboring fiefdom is a young king whose power is symbolized by the bear he leads on a chain (Chapter 7). Rather than wait for Hygmod to grow in strength and challenge him, Hrothgar takes his army to Hygmod. Hrothgar is wise enough to know that Hygmod's offer of gifts will not be sufficient to buy peace between the two rivals. But by the same token, Hygmod is smart enough to realize that his ultimate offer—the gift of his own sister, Wealtheow, as Hrothgar's bride—will not be refused. Hrothgar realizes that despite his current advantage, his kingdom is on the decline and that this new alliance may be the only way to save it.

King of the Scyldings

See Hrothgar

Lord of the Helmings

See Hygmod

Ork

The "eldest and wisest" of Hrothgar's priests by his own description, Ork is a blind prophet who encounters Grendel in Chapter 9. Ork takes his name from a recurring character in William Blake's poetry who seems to represent, at different times, Prometheus, Christ, or, in the words of critic Northrop Frye, the "dying and reviving god of [Blake's] mythology" (Frye, *Fearful Symmetry*, as quoted in Howell, *Understanding John Gardner).* Ork's eloquent and heartfelt descriptions of the principles of his philosophy puzzle Grendel. His expectations defied, the monster hesitates to murder the priest as he had planned. Among Ork's memorable descriptions of his philosophy is his description of God's purpose ("the evocation of novel intensities. He is the *lure for our feeling")* and the ultimate Evil (" 'Things fade' and 'Alternatives exclude' ").

Red Horse

Red Horse is the old peasant who is young Hrothulf's counselor. Red Horse delivers almost verbatim the anarchistic philosophy of the French thinker Georges Sorel, as written in his *Reflections on Violence* (1908). "The total ruin of institutions and morals is an act of creation. A *religious* act. Murder and mayhem are the life and soul of revolution" (Chapter 8). While Hrothulf finds some of the old man's ideas attractive, he is not completely convinced.

Scyld Shefing

Scyld Shefing is the ancient Danish King who, according to a legend, was found as a castaway by the "first men." Scyld Shefing grew up to win the "glory of men," uniting a kingdom that had been "lordless" for many years. His great deeds are still sung by the Shaper (Chapter 3).

Second priest

The second priest's main concern seems to be physical, not spiritual. He believes that he and his fellow priests should follow a strict physical regimen so that they can each put their best efforts into their daily work. Thus he scolds Ork for being outdoors at night with snow falling on him. "A man should try to be more regular," he exclaims (Chapter 9).

Shaper

The Shaper is the name the author gives to the king's poet-musician-historian, for he can shape reality just with his words. The poet is a special person in the court, who through words and music alone makes the great deeds of humanity seem even greater, thus inspiring people to take risks for what they believe in. When the blind harper in Hrothgar's court sings of the deeds of the great Scyld Shefing, "men wept like children: children sat stunned" (Chapter 3). The Shaper may manipulate the truth as much as the politician, Gardner seems to be saying.

Yet the Shaper's ability to capture the emotions of his listeners and harness their energies, so that they may live their lives in service to the highest ideals, make him higher than others in the pantheon of human heroes. When the blind singer gets old and dies, his last thought, though unfinished, suggests hope: "I see a time when the Danes once again—" (Chapter 10).

Son of Ecglaf

See Unferth

Third priest

The main concern of the third priest is with appearances, not spirituality. He worries about how Ork's behavior will affect the perception of priests by people in general. The third priest says of Ork: "Lunatic priests are bad business. They give people the willies. One man like him can turn us all to paupers" (Chapter 9).

Unferth

The bravest of the thanes in Hrothgar's court, Unferth challenges Grendel on one of his invasions of the meadhall. The monster mocks the hero's brave words, and shocks Unferth when he reveals he can speak. Instead of dignifying Unferth with combat, he throws apples at the man before leaving the hall. To Grendel's surprise, Unferth follows him home and swims through the pool above Grendel's cave to challenge his power with the hope of dying a hero. Unferth, despite his brutish side, represents the author's philosophy that "except in the life of a hero, the whole world's meaningless. The hero sees values beyond what's possible" (Chapter 6). Grendel humiliates Unferth by carrying him back to Hrothgar's meadhall alive and intact. Later in the story (Chapter 7), it is revealed that Unferth apparently murdered his brothers, an event which moved him to "put on the Shaper's idea of a hero like a merry mask." His bitter demeanor is healed by the queen's forgiveness. Despite his unresolved conflict with Grendel, Unferth remains "top man in Hrothgar's hall" (Chapter 11) until Beowulf appears. Unferth challenges the newcomer by mocking his reputation, but Beowulf refutes the story convincingly and then puts Unferth in his place by referring to his bloody past.

Wealtheow

As her description, "holy servant of common good" (Chapter 7), suggests, Wealtheow has given up her personal life for the sake of keeping peace between the Helmings and Scyldings. Though she occasionally longs for her childhood home, she never lets these feelings show to the Scyldings. In offering to sacrifice herself for the good of all, Wealtheow is a true heroine in Gardner's terms. As such, she arouses mixed feelings of love and hatred in Grendel. He resolves to kill her, but at the last moment decides against it because it would be "as meaningless as letting her live."

Artists and Society

The artist in *Grendel* is the Shaper, the court harper. His singing of great men's deeds, no matter how embellished or even falsified, renders both men and deeds immortal. Individual artists may come and go as others with greater gifts appear: this happens when the old harper in Hrothgar's hall is displaced by the Shaper, a newer and more talented bard (Chapter 3). Nevertheless, the power of art remains. While it is kings who unite countries politically, Gardner seems to be saying that they could not do so without the courage and selflessness of individuals who are inspired by the Shaper to accomplish great deeds. Such is the power of the poet that he affects even Grendel. After hearing the blind harper "sing the glory of Hrothgar's line," Grendel flees the scene, a "ridiculous hairy creature torn apart by poetry." Even though Grendel ultimately rejects the Shaper's fable, Grendel himself is still driven back to poetry in his quest to be understood. Having destroyed Hrothgar's meadhall in Chapter 6, Grendel realizes now that "as never before, I was alone." In his new role as "Wrecker of Kings," he is nothing once he runs out of kings to wreck, because "physical destruction is finite," as Howell notes. Thus later, when Grendel wants to punish Hrothgar, instead of planning some physical act of destruction, he thinks of insinuating into the king's sleep a bad dream about a "heavy blade in flight" (Chapter 8). These words (which are actually a quote from Thomas Kinsella's poem "Wormwood") are meant to evoke in the old king a nightmarish recollection of the moment he threw an ax at Grendel and began their war.

Death

There is a marked contrast in attitudes toward death between the various monsters and Beowulf and the thanes (warriors), especially Unferth. With this contrast, Gardner makes the point that personal death is insignificant to the hero if it brings a chance for immortality. For Grendel, the solipsist (one who believes nothing exists but the self), killing others means nothing. When Grendel himself faces even the slightest threat of physical harm, however, it is enough to send him wailing to his mother (Chapters 2, 12). Although Gardner embellishes the character of the dragon considerably, he does not include the scene from the original epic in which the dragon kills Beowulf. Instead, Beowulf lives to preach a gospel of death and rebirth: "The world will burn green, sperm build again. My promise. Time is the mind, the hand that makes (fingers on harpstrings, hero-swords, the acts, the eyes of queens). By that I kill you" (Chapter 12). In other words, it is through creation, imagination, and inspiration that one may kill evil and achieve immortality—even if heroic acts only live on through poetry and song.

Language and Meaning

According to Gardner, art—and especially poetry—is the only thing that gives meaning to an otherwise meaningless universe. Language is the only way that humans can break through the wall that isolates them from other humans and from the world of meaning. The wall is a recurring image in *Grendel* (see, for example, Chapters 2, 3, 8, and 12). The importance of language in *Grendel* in breaking through this wall is signaled not only by the significance of the Shaper's character but by the degree to which language plays a part in several other major characters. Most significant of these is Grendel himself, who begins the story as an inarticulate character like his mother but who rises at different points in the story to new levels of poetic intensity, however misunderstood by humans. (See, for example, Chapters 7, 8, 9, and 12.) Perhaps the most pathetic character in the story is Grendel's mother, who speaks no language at all, and who cannot even be understood by her own son. Though she does venture out of her cave at least once, to rescue her son, for the most part she is confined to a dark cave that symbolizes her total linguistic isolation.

Morals and Morality

The struggle in *Grendel* can be characterized as one between the forces of good and evil, morality and immorality. This struggle can be seen both within a single person, such as Grendel, and between individuals. Grendel, no matter how he may despise himself or seek to change, can be seen as representing the forces of evil. This would make Wealtheow and Beowulf, as well as Hrothgar and Unferth (despite their sometimes cynical or comical appearances), represent the forces of morality. Critics Helen B. Ellis and Warren U. Ober suggest in *John Gardner: Critical Perspectives* that Gardner is like the poet William Blake by implying that "the case for a particular set of values can best be made by positing an 'ironic set' of contrary values." As even Grendel recognizes, "balance is everything" (Chapter 7). Thus Hrothgar, despite his cold-blooded attempts to hold onto his throne, represents the forces of society against the threat of anarchy. We see another form of goodness in Wealtheow's comforting of the aged king, to whom she has sacrificed all personal comfort for the sake of keeping peace between potentially warring kingdoms. And of course Beowulf's slaying of Grendel at the end represents the ultimate triumph of good over evil. For Grendel, for all his artistic attempts, at the end still remains a person who believes there is no purpose in existence: a nihilist who insists that the result of his fatal fight was just an "accident" (Chapter 12) in a world with no real meaning.

Topics for Further Study

- Comment on Grendel's progress as a poet, under the influence of the Shaper, by evaluating the style and poetic effects of the doggerel he produces in Chapter 7; the verse play in Chapter 8; the free verse at the end of Chapter 9; and finally the poem in Chapter 12.

- Research the antiwar movement during the U.S. war in Vietnam, during which time *Grendel* was written. Relate the struggle between good and evil as depicted in *Grendel* to the struggle between different sectors of American society.

- Compare the philosophy of William Blake, as expressed in his poem *The Mental Traveller* and in the character of Ork, with the anarchistic philosophy of Georges Sorel, as expressed in his book *Reflections on Violence* and in the character of Red Horse, whom Gardner based on Sorel.

- Gardner added references to the twelve astrological signs to *Grendel*, focusing on one sign in each of the twelve chapters. Analyze how Gardner uses the meaning and symbolism of each astrological sign to lend unity to his overall story.

- In *Grendel*, Gardner has taken his point of departure from the classic Old English poem *Beowulf*. Compare and contrast the two stories. How are they the same? In what ways are they different?

- In *Grendel* we can see the contrast of two philosophies of government. Compare the feudal system represented by Unferth and Wealtheow in the kingdom of Hrothgar to the anarchism propounded by Red Horse, counselor to the young Hrothulf.

Point of View

Grendel is told in the first person ("I") from the point of view of the title character. Grendel is a monster with poetic aspirations whose every attempt to communicate with ordinary humans is met with misunderstanding and hostility. By focusing on the monster, the author elicits some sympathy for an otherwise thoroughly repulsive character who eats humans for pleasure. Because the point of view is that of Grendel, instead of the omniscient narrator of the original poem, the reader must deduce the story's theme from the monster's limited perspective. Fortunately Grendel is not just an aspiring poet but a good writer. In this respect he resembles Gardner's philosophical nemesis, John-Paul Sartre, whose philosophy of existentialism Gardner despised. Gardner told interviewer Marshall L. Harvey in *Chicago Review* that he wished "to present the *Beowulf* monster as Jean-Paul Sartre." According to Sartre, human beings are basically isolated individuals in an accidental world where God does not exist. Man must therefore create his own values, even though these values have no meaning outside the individual consciousness. Thus, when Grendel is attacked by the bull while trapped in a tree, he realizes that "the world was nothing: a mechanical chaos of casual, brute enmity.... I understood that, finally and absolutely, I alone exist" (Chapter 2). From that moment until the end of the story, in which Grendel describes his fatal wound as an "accident" (Chapter 12), the monster articulates Sartre's bleak philosophy.

Structure

The story begins in the "twelfth year of my idiotic war" against Hrothgar (Chapter 1) and uses the technique of flashback to tell the story of the monster's life. Grendel's long reminiscence covers from "when I was young" (Chapter 2) to the moment when he lies dying from Beowulf's fatal attack (Chapter 12). Within that frame, Gardner has ambitiously structured his tale around the twelve years of Grendel's war (one for each of the twelve chapters). He has also given each chapter an event associated with one of the twelve signs of the zodiac and their associated ruling planets and houses. (In an *American Literature* article, Barry Fawcett and Elizabeth Jones explicate each of these items.) For example, Chapter 1 opens with Aries the ram, representing Spring. Aries is associated with the planet Mars, the god of war—hence the references to Grendel's war with Hrothgar. Aries also corresponds to the first house in astrology, that of life—hence the funeral scene in which Hrothgar celebrates the life of the victims of that war. Beowulf's inspiring speech in Chapter 12, with its images of spring ("strong searching roots will crack your cave and rain will cleanse it: The world will burn green ... ") recalls the Spring imagery of

Chapter 1. In this way the author is suggesting a cyclical pattern, which reinforces Beowulf's words of rebirth. As Kathryn VanSpanckeren has analyzed at length (in *John Gardner: Critical Perspectives*), Gardner used such "embedded structures" as the narrative frame in all of his novels except *Nickel Mountain*.

Other critics, such as Craig J. Stromme in *Critique*, have noted that each chapter is designed to highlight a different school of philosophy. After Gardner's introduction to the astrological idea of endless cyclical repetition in Chapter 1, Grendel begins as a solipsist in Chapter 2—"I exist, nothing else." In Chapter 3, Grendel is exposed to the sophistry of the Shaper, who can by the power of his words make his hearers believe anything. In Chapter 4, the Shaper articulates the theology of the Old Testament, in which the children of light are contrasted to the descendants of Cain, the children of darkness. In Chapter 5, the dragon expresses English philosopher Alfred Whitehead's philosophy of the fundamental connection of all things, but Grendel can't understand it. In Chapter 6, Grendel emerges as a skeptic who, in Stromme's words, "accepts that beings other than himself exist, but… has postulated them all as enemies." Similarly, Grendel is exposed to Christianity by Wealtheow in Chapter 7, Machiavellian statecraft by Hrothulf in Chapter 8, the hypocrisy of the young priests in Chapter 9, the pessimism of Nietzsche in Chapter 10, and the nihilism of Sartre in Chapter 11. Thus *Grendel* is structured as a survey of philosophical ideas.

Parody

In Gardner's hands *Grendel* is a parody that is used both to imitate and to ridicule or admire specific pieces and forms of literature and specific authors. Most obviously, *Grendel* is a respectful tribute to its source of inspiration, the Old English classic *Beowulf.* Gardner borrows most of the plot and characters directly from the original poem. Where the author has expanded the role of a character, as in the case of Grendel or the dragon, it is generally to ridicule or act as a foil for specific philosophers and their works. For example, Grendel represents a "case history of a bad artist" whose words are constantly misunderstood by others, according to David Cowart in *Arches and Light: The Fiction of John Gardner.* He inspires only acts of violence, whereas the Shaper's words inspire hearers to do great deeds. Thus we see Grendel, inspired by the Shaper, try his own hand at poetry, which at first results in ridiculous doggerel (Chapter 7). This awkward attempt gives way to somewhat better rhymed verse (opening of Chapter 8); still more creative and metrically freer verse (end of Chapter 8); and lastly, truly inspired, alliterative verse (Chapter 12), albeit composed as Beowulf smashes Grendel against a wall. Similarly, by ridiculing the Shaper's lack of a "total vision, total system" (Chapter 5), the dragon seems to be advocating Whitehead's philosophy of connectedness, though as Howell notes, the dragon's "sneering tone seems to undercut the validity of Whitehead's vision as well as the Shaper's."

Gardner, however, is using both Grendel and the dragon in a parodic manner to bring out the prominent points of contrasting philosophies.

American Society in the Late 1960s

The heady days of the early 1960s, with their promise of peace abroad, political change in Washington, and economic boom throughout the country, had given way by the end of the decade to a series of gloomy developments. The prospect of an unwinnable war in Vietnam was compounded by numerous protests that often ended in violence. Disillusion with the American political system was symbolized by several assassinations: first, that of President John F. Kennedy in 1963, then the 1965 murder of Black Muslim leader Malcolm X, then those of Robert Kennedy and Martin Luther King, Jr. in 1968. Early advances in civil rights stood in contrast to riots by urban blacks, whose expectations had been raised but not met by President Johnson's promises of a "Great Society." Economic uncertainty was reflected in a stagnant and inflationary economy that was unable to support both the war in Vietnam and the needs of President Johnson's domestic agenda.

Protests and Politics

The 1960s saw numerous protests, particularly over issues concerning civil rights and U.S. involvement in the Vietnam War. By 1968, dissatisfaction with the Johnson administration's responses to these concerns led to a record number of protests, particularly on college campuses. Although President Lyndon Johnson declined to run for reelection in 1968, the Democratic National Convention was seen by many groups as the ideal protest forum, one which could gain them a wider audience. Several antiwar protest groups, as well as the Southern Christian Leadership Conference (SCLC), the civil-rights group once led by Dr. Martin Luther King, Jr., showed up in Chicago to protest. This led to several conflicts with Chicago police, who had been instructed by law-and-order mayor Richard Daley to stop any such protests. One legal rally led to violence when a group of police attacked not only protesters but innocent bystanders and members of the media who were covering the event. The whole conflict was captured by television cameras and broadcast nationally. In the aftermath, several leaders of activist groups—the "Chicago Seven"—were charged by the U.S. Attorney General with conspiracy to riot, even though most of them had never met before the convention.

Richard Nixon was elected president in 1968, in part aided by his "law and order" platform and his promises to bring an "honorable end" to the Vietnam War. In 1970, however, Nixon announced that U.S. military forces had invaded Cambodia, another Southeast Asian country, in order to find and destroy enemy Vietcong bases. This triggered massive demonstrations on college campuses and often rioting. The Ohio National Guard was called to quell unrest on the campus of Kent State

University, and on May 4, shots were fired into a crowd, killing four students and injuring nine others, including some students who had not even participated in the protest. Investigations later showed that, contrary to official claims, none of the victims had been physically threatening the Guards, or even been closer than sixty feet. A similar situation occurred at Jackson State University in Mississippi eleven days later, leaving two women dead. The result of these two incidents was a student strike that shut down over two hundred colleges and universities nationwide, and a country embroiled in conflict over political protest.

Compare & Contrast

- **Sixth-century A.D. Scandinavia:** Using Scandinavian chronicles and sagas, it is possible to date the historical events in the original *Beowulf*, the basis for *Grendel*, to this time and place. The basic political conflict in *Beowulf* is between the Danes (represented by Hrothgar's house) and the Geats (represented by Beowulf and his visiting party). Similarly, the rivalry between Hrothgar and Hrothulf over what would happen to the throne when Hrothgar died are also recounted in the Scandinavian analogues.

1960s-1970s United States: Political turmoil in the United States reaches a peak with students protesting the Vietnam War at the Democratic National Convention in Chicago in 1968. The Chicago police, under Democratic Mayor Richard Daley, repress the demonstrations with great force, leading to disillusionment not only in the Democratic Party (whose candidate, Hubert Humphrey, eventually lost the presidential election to Richard Nixon) but also in the whole democratic process.

Today: Widespread disillusionment with the political process continues, with record numbers of eligible voters not voting and widespread cynicism among both politicians and voters about the effectiveness of the democratic process. Today, cynicism feeds on the controversy surrounding the ways in which political campaigns and candidates are financed. Cynicism also flourishes because of the decrease in bipartisan spirit on many issues between the two major political parties. Nevertheless, there is agreement that the U.S. system of government still seems to work as well or better than any system others have been able to devise.

- **Sixth-century A.D. Scandinavia:** The political tribes of the area have little interaction with cultures outside of Europe; the fall of the Roman Empire in 476 A.D., while creating new political realities throughout Europe, is scarcely felt in Scandinavia (which had never been a part of the Roman Empire) either politically or economically.

1960s-1970s United States: This period sees the beginning of an increasingly inflationary economy (where prices rise quickly). The high inflation of this stagnant economy, combined with the oil embargo by Arab nations, produces a serious economic recession in 1973 and 1974.

Today: Fueled by low inflation and interest rates, the steady growth of the U.S. economy leads to a period of economic prosperity and optimism unequaled since the early 1960s. In 1997 the influence of a worldwide economy can be seen in a sudden drop in the U.S. stock market, caused by economic downturns in Asian countries.

- **Sixth-century A.D. Scandinavia:**

Power rests on wealth from raids and trading, although trading eastward is cut off during this period by the Huns and Avars. Society consists of a landed aristocracy and farmer tenants and a local court system.

1960s-1970s United States: Young people, particularly students, challenge the authority of those who govern at all levels. There is a general questioning of the right of a power elite, composed largely of white males, to make policy for an increasingly younger and more diverse citizenry. Civil rights groups continue to fight for the rights of minorities, while others focus on equal rights for women and homosexuals.

Today: There is a greater representation of women and minorities in various areas of life, including government and the workforce. Nevertheless, some inequalities remain, particularly economic ones, and racial issues are prominent in politics. A country containing individuals of diverse social, sexual, and ethnic identities, the United States remains more a "salad bowl" of many separate ingredients rather than a "melting pot" containing one definition of "American."

Literature of the 1960s

As befitted an era of conflict and protest, much of the literature of the 1960s was concerned with political issues. Socially conscious artists saw their work as a means to communicate their ideas, criticisms, and protests. Black humor, such as that found in the antiwar novels *Slaughterhouse-Five* by Kurt Vonnegut or *Catch-22* by Joseph Heller, was often employed to satirize issues of the day. Writers also experimented with form, trying new and different techniques to push the boundaries of traditional fiction. These more literary works often ended up on best-seller lists, adopted by a reading public open to new literary possibilities and new ideas. By the end of the 1960s, however, many artists became frustrated with what they felt was a lack of effectiveness in using art to achieve social reform. They adopted a nihilistic viewpoint—that existence is pointless. Literary works reflected this view either by focusing only on a work's form, not its content, or by using absurdity to deal with the hopelessness of life.

Gardner's *Grendel*, written at the tail end of this era, attempted to refute this nihilistic viewpoint. While the twelve-chapter structure is an important part of the novel, this form serves to highlight and support the content, not replace it. Gardner also makes an argument for the importance of the artist in society. Through the character of the Shaper, the author points out the positive influence an artist may have on those around him. In this way, Gardner's work reflects the spirit of many other literary novels of the day, and achieved similar success.

Critical Overview

Gardner's first two published novels, *The Resurrection* (1966) and *The Wreckage of Agathon* (1970) generated little response, although Geoffrey Wolff did praise the latter in *Newsweek*. With *Grendel* (1971), however, as David Cowart noted in *Arches and Light*, "the critical tide of caution began to turn. Reviewers were charmed, and *Time* and *Newsweek* cited it among the year's best novels. After a first printing of 7500 copies, it went through nine hardback and thirteen paperback printings in this country and England by the end of 1977. It had also, by then, been translated into French, Spanish, and Swedish." No doubt some of this attention was due to readers' familiarity with Grendel's literary source, the classic epic poem *Beowulf*, known especially to high school and college English students and their professors. Academics in particular respected the author, who was already an established scholar in medieval studies, having edited four books and translated two other works in this field.

But critics generally also felt, as David Cowart wrote in the *Dictionary of Literary Biography*, that in *Grendel* Gardner "burnishes the classic at the same time that he creates a new masterpiece." Academic critics in particular responded to Gardner's scholarship in drawing not only on medieval sources but also poets from William Blake to Thomas Kinsella and philosophers from Plato to

Whitehead and Sartre. Critics also relished unravelling the novel's structure, with its allusions to the signs of the zodiac and various school of philosophical thought. The character of Grendel received special attention, with a lively debate ensuing over whether that monster, who is certainly the central character in the story, is not also its real hero. Like the Shaper, Grendel is engaged in a struggle to create poetry. (As these critics noted, Beowulf, the ostensible hero of the novel, makes only a relatively brief appearance toward the end.) Some critics went as far as to consider Grendel an absurd hero whose violent nihilism is the only sane reaction to the chaos of modern society.

Gardner himself lent insight into this debate in his treatise *On Moral Fiction.* In this 1978 work (which according to *New York Times Magazine* contributor Stephen Singular was actually written in 1965), Gardner criticized contemporary novelists like Saul Bellow, John Barth, John Updike, and Thomas Pynchon for not practicing "moral art." By this term he meant art which "in its highest form holds up models of virtue, whether they be heroic models like Homer's Achilles or models of quiet endurance like the coal miners ... in the photographs of W. Eugene Smith." In a similar vein, a year earlier Gardner had told *Atlantic Monthly* interviewers Don Edwards and Carol Polsgrove that "if we celebrate bad values in our arts, we're going to have a bad society. If we celebrate values which make you healthier, which make life better, we're going to have a better world." These statements would seem to indicate the author's intent lay in rebuking Grendel's nihilist viewpoints. That the work has been interpreted in exactly the opposite fashion is, according to various critics, either a testament to Gardner's ability to invent a powerful and sympathetic protagonist or an indication of his problems in clearly presenting his ideas.

Despite the fervency and highmindedness of such views, *On Modern Fiction* elicited mostly negative reactions from both reviewers and fellow writers, as summarized by Cowart in *Arches and Light.* Not surprisingly, the novelists who were attacked in the essay fought back in print in widely read forums like the *New York Times.* And since Gardner had boldly and unapologetically set a high standard for artists, his own novels, especially his later ones, were soon being judged by this same standard and found wanting. Critic John Romano, for example, claimed in the *New York Times Book Review* that *Freddy's Book* (1980) wasn't moral since its exuberance threatened to "slip over into immorality at any turn" and that Gardner's moral aesthetic contradicted his medievalist love for "the fabulous, the enchanted."

Thus far, however, Gardner's *Grendel* has, for the most part, escaped such criticism. As Fawcett and Jones stated in *American Literature*, "Somewhere in our cavernous hearts the old heroic ideals continue to haunt and illumine us. Grendel's conflict, as he holds fast to skepticism yet sways toward vision, turning and twisting between mockery and anguish, poetry and black humor, continually ironizing his ironies, is our own as inhabitants of the twentieth century."

What Do I Read Next?

- *Beowulf is* the oldest epic narrative in any modern European language. As the major inspiration for Gardner's *Grendel*, it will be of great interest to any reader who enjoyed Gardner's version. One of several good translations is that by Charles W. Kennedy (Oxford University Press, 1940). It also contains a helpful introduction with sections on historical background, the history of the manuscript itself, and the influence of the classical epic and various folk sources.

- Gardner's best-known nonfiction work, *On Moral Fiction* (1978), is concerned with the purpose and craft of fiction and is basically a statement of Gardner's philosophy. Passionate, blunt in tone, and sometimes contradictory, it found favor with those who agreed with the author about the essential humanity of great literature. Nevertheless, Gardner riled some critics who felt that his judgments on some of his fellow contemporary novelists were too harsh.

- Gardner's *The Sunlight Dialogues* (1972) explores on a massive scale the theme of order versus chaos, with eighty characters and an intricate plot set in Gardner's hometown of Batavia, New York. In this novel, described by David Cowart in the *Dictionary of Literary Biography* as "possibly his finest," Gardner sets in opposition the Sunlight Man, a mercurial and mysterious criminal who represents absolute freedom, and Fred Clumly, a local police officer who espouses law and order.

- *The Legacy of Heorot* (1987) is a science-fiction version of the first part of *Beowulf* that is set on Earth's first stellar colony. The spot seems like paradise, until dogs and cattle begin to disappear, devoured by a monster. Authors Larry Niven, Jerry Pournelle, and Steven Barnes have combined forces to create a frighteningly realistic horror story à la Stephen King.

Sources

David Cowart, "John Champlin Gardner, Jr.," in *Dictionary of Literary Biography*, Vol. 2: *American Novelists since World War II*, edited by Jeffrey Helterman and Richard Layman, Gale, 1978, p. 177.

David Cowart, *Arches & Light: The Fiction of John Gardner*, Southern Illinois University Press, 1983.

Don Edwards and Carol Polsgrove, "A Conversation with John Gardner," in *Atlantic Monthly*, May, 1977, p. 43.

Helen B. Ellis and Warren U. Ober, "'Grendel' and Blake: The Contraries of Existence," in *John Gardner: Critical Perspectives*, edited by Robert A. Morace and Kathryn VanSpanckeren, Southern Illinois University Press, 1982, p. 47.

Barry Fawcett and Elizabeth Jones, "The Twelve Traps in John Gardner's *Grendel,"* in *American Literature*, Vol. 62, December, 1990, pp. 634-647.

John Gardner, *On Moral Fiction*, Basic Books, 1978, p. 82.

Marshall L. Harvey, "Where Philosophy and Fiction Meet: An Interview with John Gardner," in *Chicago Review*, Vol. 29, Spring, 1978, p. 75.

John M. Howell, *Understanding John Gardner*, University of South Carolina Press, 1993, pp. 61, 71-73.

John Romano, review of *Freddy's Book*, in *New*

York Times Book Review,, March 23, 1980, p. 26.

Stephen Singular, "The Sound and Fury over Fiction," in *New York Times Magazine*, July 8, 1979, p. 36.

Craig J. Stromme, "The Twelve Chapters of *Grendel,"* in *Critique*, Vol. 20, No. 1, 1978, p. 87.

Kathryn VanSpanckeren, "Magical Prisons: Embedded Structures in the Work of John Gardner," in *John Gardner: Critical Perspectives*, edited by Robert A. Morace and Kathryn VanSpanckeren, Southern Illinois University Press, 1982, pp. 114-129.

For Further Study

Leonard Butts, "The Monster as Artist: *Grendel* and *Freddy's Book,"* in his *The Novels of John Gardner: Making Life Art as a Moral Process*, Louisiana State University Press, 1983, pp. 86-110.

> Butts discusses Grendel as a failed artist who lives in his own first-person narrative, unable to make connections with humans or redeem himself through imagination and art.

Norma L. Hutman, "Even Monsters Have Mothers: A Study of 'Beowulf and John Gardner's 'Grendel,'" in *MOSAIC: A Journal for the Comparative Study of Literature and Ideas*, Vol. 9, No. 1, 1975, pp. 19-31.

> The author compares the two works and finds that Gardner's novel stands up well beside the older classic.

Jerome Klinkowitz, "John Gardner's 'Grendel,'" in *John Gardner: Critical Perspectives*, edited by Robert A. Morace and Kathryn VanSpanckeren, Southern Illinois University Press, 1982, pp. 62-67.

> Characterizes the work as a product of its times and faults it for being Gardner's personal experiment instead of addressing its real audience.

Dean McWilliams, *"Grendel,"* in his *John Gardner*,

Twayne, 1990, pp. 29-41.

> McWilliams reads *Grendel* as an exploration of the role of dialogue in the creation of the self and the world.

Joseph Milosh, "John Gardner's *Grendel* : Sources and Analogues," in *Contemporary Literature*, Vol. 19, No. 1, Winter, 1978, pp. 48-57.

> An essay connecting *Grendel* with Chaucer's *The Nun's Priest's Tale.*

Jay Rudd, "Gardner's Grendel and *Beowulf:* Humanizing the Monster," in *THOTH*, Spring/Fall, 1974, pp. 3-17.

> A close analysis of the original poem and why it is so appealing to modern writers like Barth, Heller, and Beckett, as well as Gardner.

Printed in the USA
CPSIA information can be obtained
at www.ICGtesting.com
LVHW010544231123
764666LV00010B/1190